W9-BUO-707

essential careers™

A CAREER AS AN
ATHLETIC
TRAINER

MARY-LANE KAMBERG

ROSEN
PUBLISHING®

NEW YORK

For Coach Eric Falls

Published in 2013 by The Rosen Publishing Group, Inc.
29 East 21st Street, New York, NY 10010

Copyright © 2013 by The Rosen Publishing Group, Inc.

First Edition

Library of Congress Cataloging-in-Publication Data

Kamberg, Mary-Lane, 1948–
A career as an athletic trainer/Mary-Lane Kamberg.—1st ed.
    p. cm.—(Essential careers)
Includes bibliographical references and index.
ISBN 978-1-4488-8238-0 (library binding)
1. Athletic trainers—Training of—United States. 2. Athletics—Vocational guidance—Juvenile literature. I. Title.
RC1210.K36 2013
796.092—dc23
[B]

2012016423

Manufactured in the United States of America

CPSIA Compliance Information: Batch #W13YA: For further information, contact Rosen Publishing, New York, New York, at 1-800-237-9932.

contents

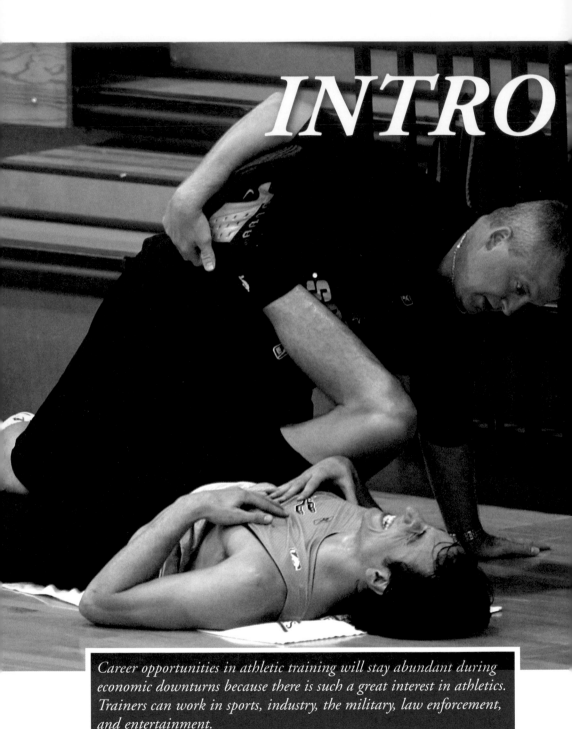

INTRO

Career opportunities in athletic training will stay abundant during economic downturns because there is such a great interest in athletics. Trainers can work in sports, industry, the military, law enforcement, and entertainment.

DUCTION

L ooking for a job can be hard. Choosing a career is harder. A job may last only a few years. A career can last a lifetime.

When you choose a career, you want to take into account what you'd like to do. You also need to think about whether the career will stay strong during tough economic times. Will you stand in the unemployment line? Or will your field of work stay important no matter the financial state of the nation?

Athletic training is one career that will. Athletic trainers work in sports medicine. They are part of a team of members of the health care industry. Sports injuries can cause serious pain. They can result in permanent disability or even death. Helping athletes or others keep from getting hurt is a main part of a trainer's job. So is helping them recover.

The first team doctors in America began working in colleges in the mid-1950s. Since then, the field of sports medicine has grown. Today, athletic trainers are an important part of the sports medicine team, with many job opportunities. Most trainers work in sports. You see them at all levels, from youth clubs to schools to the pros. But some work in industry, public safety, the armed forces, and the performing arts.

Using trainers pays off. It improves productivity. It also saves money for health care and insurance. So teams and companies will still employ trainers even if they have to lay off other workers. The National Athletic Trainers' Association (NATA) in Dallas, Texas, is the professional association for certified athletic trainers.

A 2008 NATA study found that trainers working in business and industry give their employers a good return on investment. That means the trainers saved the companies more than it cost to hire them. All of the companies that kept records said they had a good return on investment. More than 80 percent of them saved at least $3 for each dollar spent. The study also found that work-related injuries

People who would make good athletic trainers have an interest in sports and human motion. They also want a career where they can help others.

went down at least 25 percent in 85 percent of companies using trainers.

In 2011, the U.S. Bureau of Labor Statistics said that most athletic trainers have full-time jobs with benefits. But the job duties will continue to evolve, and the bureau thinks the career of athletic training will change over the next ten years. The changes may include more administrative duties, new technology, and working with more patients. Trainers must be able to adapt to these changes. For up-to-date information about salaries and athletic training as a career, visit the bureau's Web site (http://www.bls.gov).

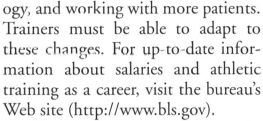

Choosing a career means matching your likes and interests to a type of work. When those go together, you'll have a job that makes you want to go to work. If you are interested in sports and the way the body moves, and if you want a career where you can help others, you would make a good athletic trainer.

chapter 1

WHAT ATHLETIC TRAINERS DO

A basketball point guard takes a pre-season fitness test. A dance team member dislocates her kneecap in a half-time show. A quarterback wants to play again after shoulder surgery.

Wherever you find athletes, you'll find certified athletic trainers. They help players prevent, treat, and recover from injuries.

"Our job is to return the athlete to the game as safely and quickly as possible," says Wayne Harmon. He is a certified athletic trainer in Olathe, Kansas. He has worked with minor league baseball players. He has also worked with colleges and high schools.

Prevention starts before the sports season. The best way to prevent injury is to get in shape. Another is to use the right skills for the sport. Athletic trainers teach athletes, coaches, and parents how to keep from getting hurt.

Athletic trainers conduct preseason tests. The goal of these exams is to reduce the risk of injury.

Athletic trainers identify and treat injuries, sometimes on the field during a game. However, another important part of the job is preventing those injuries in the first place.

Preseason screening of an athlete's strength, flexibility, endurance, and general fitness can find weaknesses. The athlete can strengthen those areas in order to prevent sports injuries.

PRESEASON TESTING

A preseason screening looks at vision, heart, lungs, bones, joints, and the brain. It also tests for flexibility. Screenings may also include tests of the blood and urine, pulse rate, and blood pressure. Doctors review the results and decide if an athlete can play a particular sport.

Some conditions call for strength training. The player may need a brace for a weak joint. Some conditions keep an athlete out of sports. Others may let the athlete play one sport but not another.

For example, suppose a gymnast falls and breaks a bone in her back. After the bone heals, a doctor may keep her out of gymnastics. But the doctor could let her join the swim team. Another fall in gymnasts could result in paralysis. But swimming has a much lower chance of accidents.

The doctor thinks about many issues. Will the athlete risk injury? Could other players get hurt? Can the athlete practice and play if he or she takes medicine or uses a brace? Can the athlete play within limits?

Each case is different. But in general, doctors and other members of the sports medicine team agree. They lean toward letting athletes play. But playing must not risk their health.

The preseason examination may also include tests of each athlete's strength, flexibility, endurance, and general fitness. This spots weak areas. Results help sports trainers design an exercise program to make these areas strong. Many college and professional teams hire special strength and conditioning coaches for this use.

PROTECTIVE EQUIPMENT

Another way to prevent injury is the use of equipment that protects players in the sport. Helmets, padding, shin guards, knee pads, and mouth guards protect the head, shoulders, legs, knees, and teeth. Trainers must know the needed equipment for each sport they work with.

The National Operating Committee on Standards for Athletic Equipment (NOCSAE) issues the standards in the United States. It makes rules for helmets for batting, lacrosse, and football. It also covers face masks, baseballs, and softballs. The NOCSAE symbol indicates the item meets these standards. Other groups also rule on sporting equipment. These include the Canadian Standards Association, the European Standards Association, and the Hockey Equipment Certification Council.

Some groups work on rules to make sports safer. Two are the American Medical Association's Committee on the Medical Aspects of Sports and

the National Collegiate Athletics Association (NCAA) Committee on Competitive Standards of Sports.

The groups require some types of equipment. They recommend others. They also ban some. Illegal equipment increases the risk of injury to the player, teammates, or the other team. In basketball, for example, players may not wear a cast below the elbow. Braces must be flexible and not made from plaster or metal.

PROTECTIVE TAPES AND WRAPS

Athletic adhesive tape and elastic wraps are important items in an athletic trainer's toolbox. Athletic trainers use them

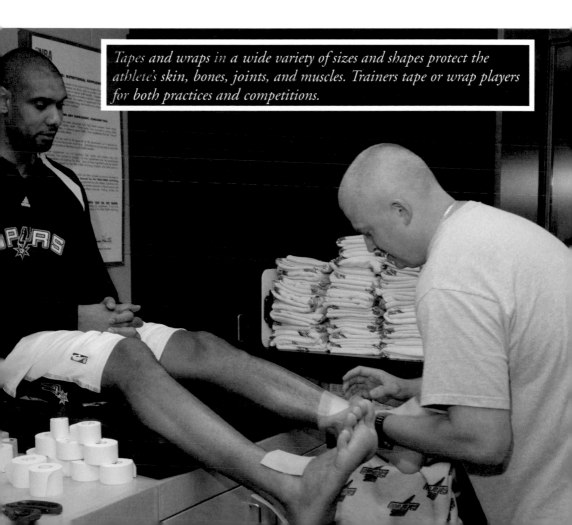

Tapes and wraps in a wide variety of sizes and shapes protect the athlete's skin, bones, joints, and muscles. Trainers tape or wrap players for both practices and competitions.

for both practice and games. It depends on why they are needed. Tapes and wraps have many uses. They protect the athlete's skin, bones, joints, and muscles. They keep a part of the body from moving. Or they support a weak joint. Tapes and wraps do the following:

- Close cuts
- Prevent blisters
- Keep pads, bandages, and splints in place
- Support joints, arms, and legs
- Ease stress on ligaments
- Apply pressure to an injury
- Restrict motion

EMERGENCY CARE

In January 2012, former Florida Panthers right wing Richard Zednik was in his home country of Slovakia. He was teaching young ice hockey players at a skating rink in Námestovo. Earlier, ice and heavy snow had piled on the roof. Without warning, the roof fell in. The players made it safely off the ice just after the first pieces fell. No one was hurt. But the danger of multiple injuries was high. If anyone was hurt, an athletic trainer would have been called upon at once.

Trainers don't just sit around and wait for someone to get hurt. One of their tasks is to develop a crisis plan for emergencies. A crisis plan is also called an emergency care plan. It states who is in charge of what in an emergency. The NATA says every sports organization needs a written emergency plan—before a crisis occurs.

The trainer makes the plan. But he or she needs ideas from the main members of the sports medicine team. Trainers also talk with people from the community's emergency medical services and hospitals. For school sports, principals, athletic directors, and lawyers should help with the plan. They should also review it before putting it into place.

THE CRISIS PLAN

A good emergency plan answers eighteen questions:
1. Who will evaluate the injury and start first aid?
2. Is a list of up-to-date emergency phone numbers available?
3. Who will call 911?
4. Who will control the crowd?
5. Which supplies are needed and who will bring them?
6. Who will move the athlete away from the scene?
7. How can emergency services easily and safely get to the area?
8. Who will meet the ambulance and guide the first responders to the scene?
9. Who will contact the injured athlete's parents?
10. If more than one athlete is hurt, where will personnel sort them by how serious each injury is?
11. Who can help in case of a major casualty and how can the trainer reach them?
12. Who will fill out accident reports and talk to people who saw what happened?
13. What might get in the way of the ambulance crew? How can the trainer remove these items or make them easier to deal with?
14. How does the plan apply to different sports? Are changes needed for such areas as pools, gyms, and outdoor fields?
15. How will people who are "just looking" be moved from the area?
16. Where is the crisis plan located?

THE SPORTS MEDICINE TEAM

Certified athletic trainers work as a team with other sports medicine professionals, including:

- Doctors, who specialize in injuries to the skeleton, muscles, joints, and tissues
- Massage therapists, who work soft tissues to prevent or ease pain
- Sports nutritionists, for diet related to best performance
- Physical therapists, for special exercises to regain or improve physical abilities
- Sport psychologists, who deal with psychological and mental issues
- Others, including the athlete, parent, and coach

17. Who will talk to the media?
18. Who will offer grief counseling or other therapy if needed?

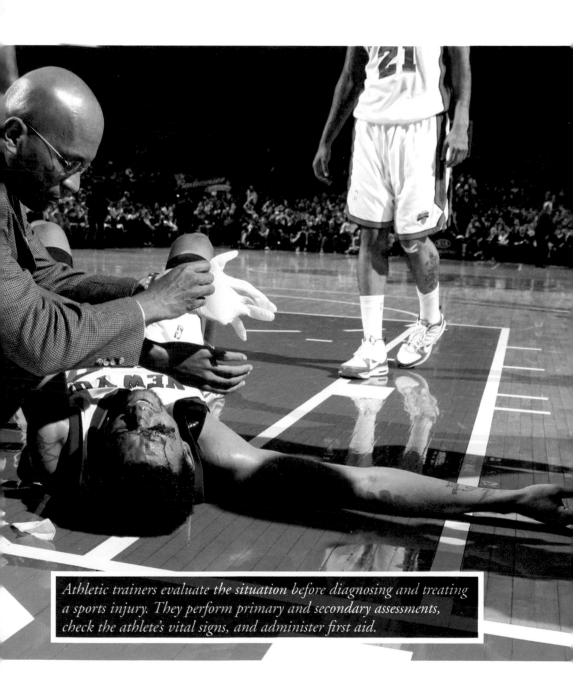

Athletic trainers evaluate the situation before diagnosing and treating a sports injury. They perform primary and secondary assessments, check the athlete's vital signs, and administer first aid.

Making a plan is not enough. Everyone must practice together. The athletic trainer often is the one who schedules these dry runs.

INJURY EVALUATION AND FIRST AID

A diver hits the board during the state championship meet. He is bleeding and floating facedown in the water. What happens next?

Athletic trainers are often the first to get to an injured athlete. Their first priority is to evaluate the situation. What happened? Is any danger present?

The trainer then performs a primary assessment. This is a check for consciousness and signs of life-threatening injuries. Can the injured athlete respond to directions? Answer questions? If not, the trainer goes to the ABCs of first aid. He or she checks for life-threatening injuries to the airway (A), breathing (B), and circulation (C). If the athlete can talk, he or she clearly can breathe and has a heartbeat. After that, the trainer checks for bleeding. Any problems noted in the primary assessment are treated first.

After that, the trainer does a secondary assessment. This includes getting information about the athlete's medical history. A medical history is a record of past and present health. How does the history affect the current state of health? Has the athlete had previous injury to this part of the body? What other medical conditions are present? Once the history is known, the trainer checks (in this order) the head, vital signs, arms, chest, abdomen, hips, and legs.

Vital signs include body temperature, skin color, breathing rate, and heart rate. They also involve response to pain, reaction of the pupils of the eyes, ability to move, and capillary refill. Capillary refill is the time it takes for blood to return to the fingertip after the trainer presses on the fingernail and then releases pressure. Slow refill may mean poor blood supply. The trainer may also check blood pressure and breath sounds.

Certified athletic trainers diagnose injuries. They provide emergency care, including first aid and cardiopulmonary resuscitation (CPR). Athletic trainers often provide the first treatment of an injury. They also coordinate care with doctors and other members of the sports medicine team.

Athletes with serious injuries may need a doctor's care. Such care may include drugs, casts, surgery, or other treatment. For example, a basketball player may need surgery to repair a torn anterior cruciate ligament (ACL). The ACL is one of the four main ligaments in the knee. Ligaments are tissues that attach a bone to a bone. The ACL connects the back of the thighbone to the front of the shinbone. A torn ACL is often seen in contact sports like football. It's also seen in sports like basketball, where athletes twist or make fast changes of direction.

GETTING ATHLETES BACK IN THE GAME

Once an injury starts to heal, most athletes want to get back in the game. Trainers work with a plan to make that happen as soon as safely possible. Trainers may use massage, hot or cold packs, or other treatments. The plan may also include braces and wraps. Athletes with long recovery times often need to rebuild strength and endurance. They must be able to move the joint in all directions. They also need to be able to stretch out the muscles. Athletic trainers have ways to help do that. Trainers also teach how to build strength, endurance, speed, and power, and they help athletes regain skills they need for their specific sports.

The sports medicine team then decides when the athlete can return first to modified practice, then to full practice and competition. In some cases, the recovery plan sends the athlete back on the field in better shape than before he or she was injured.

chapter 2

WHY SPORTS INJURIES MATTER

B efore a December 10, 2011, college basketball game, two star athletes had painful injuries. They each had the same decision to make—"Will I play?"

The Ohio State Buckeyes' forward/center Jared Sullinger had already missed one game due to back spasms. He sat out practice all week. The training staff hesitated to clear him for the game. His coach, Thad Matta, said, "I'm never going to jeopardize one of my players' futures." At the time, Ohio State was second in the national rankings. They wanted to be national champions. The team had already beaten Duke and the University of Florida. They did not have to beat the University of Kansas to reach their season goal. Sullinger sat on the bench for the game.

In the home team's locker room, the Jayhawk training staff worried about guard Tyshawn Taylor's knee. In practice five days earlier, he sprained the tissue that connects the thighbone to the shin. He had also torn cartilage in the knee. Cartilage forms a cushion between joints. When Taylor got hurt, the sports medicine team wanted to rush him to surgery.

Taylor refused. His team was ranked thirteenth. He insisted on playing in the game. During the off-season he had pegged the Ohio State game a "must win." He delayed surgery until the day after the game. He played with the pain. Still, he had a career-high thirteen assists. That tied for fifth in Kansas history in a

Jared Sullinger of the Ohio State Buckeyes attempts a shot in a January 2012 game against Indiana University. He was cleared to play after healing from an earlier back injury.

single game. Kansas won the game 78–67. Jayhawks coach Bill Self, talking about Taylor, said, "Without him, we don't win."

THE EFFECT OF SPORTS INJURIES

Sports injuries matter—not only to athletes, but also to their families, teams, and coaches. Injuries also affect health care workers and insurance companies.

Athletes want to know how long they'll be out of their sports. They also want to know if they can ever get back to their pre-injury conditions. Some injuries can end a player's season. Or career. And some injuries have lifelong effects. A former football lineman with a bad hip, for example, might have years of pain after his playing days are over.

An injury can also limit an athlete's career and future income. A high school player can lose a college scholarship. A college player might be unable to go pro. And a professional player can lose money in trades or future contracts. A pro can also lose deals to advertise products and services.

Children who get hurt in sports can give up or reduce other physical activity, according to a study by the NATA. And an injury can affect the young athlete's life outside of sports. The study also found that injuries in youth can lead to health problems in later life.

EFFECTS ON FAMILIES, TEAMS, AND COACHES

Sports injuries also upset the lives of family members. The child's school and sports routines change. So do parents' work schedules. Almost one-third of parents whose child athletes are hurt take time off work to care for them, says Jennifer L. Minigh in *Sports Medicine*. For adults who provide all or part of a family's income, a sports injury can cause missed work and lost income. Family members may have to adjust their daily lives to care for the adult athlete at home.

When a player is hurt, so is the team. If the injury happens in a game, teammates might seek revenge on the other team. Or teammates may play with fear that they, too, will get hurt. Loss of a player can reduce the chance of a win or a championship. Coaches must keep the other players focused on the game. And they may have to change game strategy. Coaches may also have to be part of the injured athlete's recovery plan.

HEALTH CARE AND INSURANCE COSTS

Research offers new technologies to diagnose and treat sports injury. But they come with a price. Sports injuries

ANCIENT SPORTS MEDICINE

Ancient Greeks and Romans were the earliest sports medicine professionals. A sixth century BCE wrestler named Milo of Croton was the first to urge athletes to use progressive resistance training. This is a way to build muscle strength. The method increases weight and number of repetitions over time. Milo told athletes to "lift a bull every day starting from the day of the bull's birth." Milo said the athletes could then lift the full-grown bull.

Iccus of Tarentum was an athlete from an ancient city near Rome, Italy. He wrote the first textbook on athletic training in 444 BCE. He supported the use of diet and exercise to maintain health. The original book is lost, but several later texts that survive refer to the book and Iccus's ideas.

In the second century CE, the physician Galen was the first team doctor—for gladiators.

Participating in such extreme sports as scuba diving, skydiving, climbing, and motor racing can increase the cost of life insurance premiums because of the danger involved.

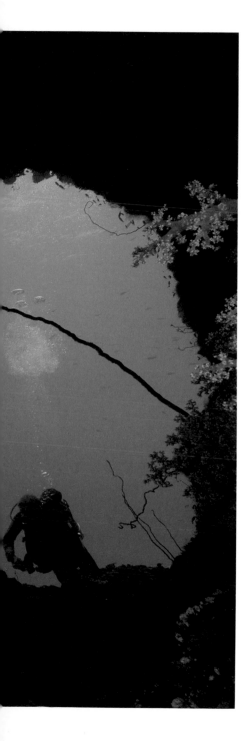

raise health care costs. It follows that the cost of insurance also goes up. Health insurance must cover the higher and higher costs.

The risk of harm from sports makes life insurance costs rise, too. They rise even higher if a person participates in extreme sports. They also rise for such dangerous sports as scuba diving, skydiving, climbing, and motor racing.

Sports injuries also affect the price of malpractice insurance. Malpractice is negligence that hurts someone. In legal terms, negligence is failure to provide reasonable care. Hospitals and health care workers buy this type of insurance to cover the cost of being sued if a patient has a bad result.

COMMON SPORTS INJURIES

Injuries happen in practice and games. They occur during the preseason, season, and post-season. The NCAA studied fifteen college sports between 1988 and 2004. The study covered game and practice injuries. To be counted, the injury had to need medical care. And the athlete had to miss at least one day of practice. The study also defined "athlete exposure." That meant one athlete playing in one game or practice. The study involved 182,000 injuries and 1 million athlete exposures.

The study found that injuries happened in games much more often than in practices. The numbers below are the number of injuries per 1,000 exposures. In games, the rate was 13.8. In practices, the rate was 4. The rate for preseason practice was a lot higher than that for in-season and postseason. The preseason rate was 6.6. The in-season rate was 2.3. The postseason rate was 1.4.

Football had the highest rates in both games and practices. In games, football players had 35.9 injuries. In practices, the rate was 9.6. Women's softball had the lowest rate in games (4.3). Men's baseball had the lowest in practice (1.9).

The percentages in all categories changed very little over the sixteen years.

Today, the NCAA still keeps track of sports injuries. The information helps it see what it can do to reduce the numbers.

WHERE DOES IT HURT?

The NCAA study found that more than half of all sports injuries were to the legs and feet. Sprained ankles accounted for 15 percent of all injuries. Over the years the data showed a big increase in both ACL injuries and concussions. Researchers thought the rise was due in part to better ways to identify the injuries, not necessarily more injuries.

Young athletes also get hurt in sports. According to the Centers for Disease Control and Prevention (CDC), more than 3.5 million children under the age of fifteen are treated for

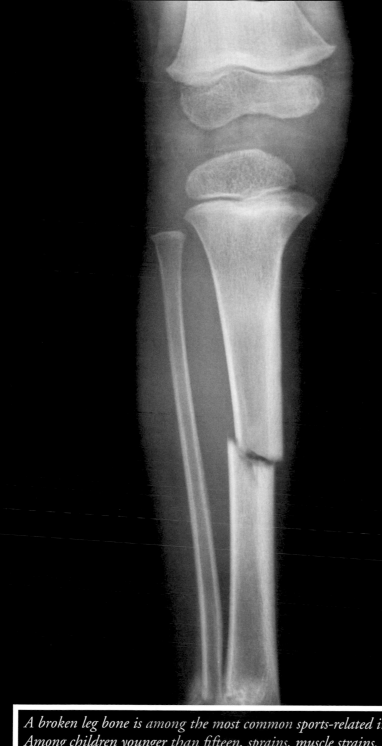

A broken leg bone is among the most common sports-related injuries. Among children younger than fifteen, sprains, muscle strains, and growth plate injuries are also common.

sports injuries each year. The most common ones are sprains, muscle strains, and bone and growth plate injuries.

According to *USA Today*, an estimated twelve million American athletes between ages five and twenty-two annually lose twenty million school days. Their health care costs reach $33 billion per year.

Sports injuries also cause trouble for active adults. As the body ages, it loses its ability to move. It also loses the ability to make fast changes of direction. Recovery may take longer than that for young people. Adults with inactive lifestyles also risk getting hurt when they try to get more active too fast.

ACUTE AND CHRONIC INJURIES

Injuries are either acute or chronic. Acute injuries occur at once. Signs are sudden, severe pain; swelling; tenderness; weakness; inability to put weight on a leg; and inability to move a joint. Acute injuries also include a dislocated or broken bone. Some acute injuries are sprained ankles, broken fingers, and concussions.

Chronic injuries come from activity over a longer time. They are caused by too much use or repeated motion. They cause a dull ache during rest. They cause pain during exercise. They can also cause swelling. Golfers often get chronic injuries to the lower back, shoulders, and ankles. Tennis players get tennis elbow. That comes from small tears in the tendon over time. A tendon is the part of a muscle that attaches to a bone.

Athletic injuries can happen to any part of the body. So trainers need a basic knowledge of the human body. Among the most common places hurt include the shoulder, knee, head, and spine. Organ damage most often occurs to the spleen, liver, and kidney.

For the trainer, every injury is new. "The injury itself and the circumstances surrounding it are unique and ever changing," says Robbie Dyson, a certified athletic trainer at Verrado High School in Buckeye, Arizona. "Two people may come to you with what appears to be quite similar injuries. But these same two people have very different experiences. Treatment has to be different in terms of the injury and the goals of the person being treated."

SPORTS MEDICINE BENEFITS EVERYONE

Research and technology help athletes and nonathletes alike. Research into nutrition for athletes can find facts about diet's role in general health. And other research studies have resulted in better helmets, lighter shoes, and stronger bats and racquets.

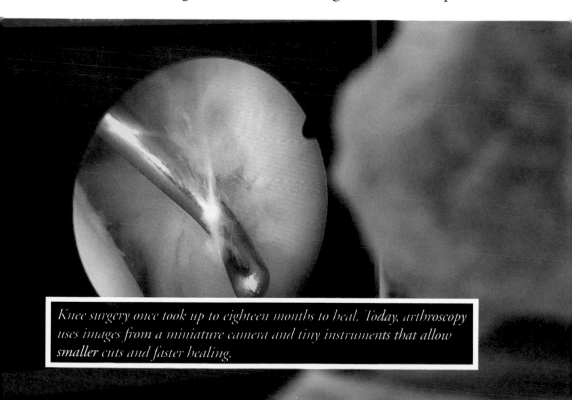

Knee surgery once took up to eighteen months to heal. Today, arthroscopy uses images from a miniature camera and tiny instruments that allow smaller cuts and faster healing.

Better design has created faster skates and skis, as well as improved wheelchairs.

New technology, such as better imaging, helps doctors diagnose problems. For example, digital 3-D reconstruction creates a three-dimensional digital picture that accurately shows an injury.

New surgical techniques help patients heal faster and more completely. For example, arthroscopy is a surgical technique used to diagnose and treat joint problems.

The way the surgery is done has changed. In the past, doctors needed a long cut to open the knee. This type of surgery is called open surgery. It is the traditional type of operation. The doctor sees the body structure and inserts instruments through the long opening. However, in most cases, the longer the cut, the longer the knee takes to heal.

Today, surgeons use arthroscopy to diagnose and treat knee problems. This method takes advantage of better views of the area to be repaired. The better views come from miniature cameras. They send enlarged images to a monitor. At first the method was used only for diagnosis. Now surgeons use tiny instruments. The small tools fit through the small cuts around the knee. The smaller cuts take less time to heal.

"Recovery from ACL surgery used to take eighteen months," says Wayne Harmon of Kansas. "Today, players are back in the game in six months."

Thirty years ago, a patient who had ACL surgery had to keep the leg straight for three months. Today, the patient moves the leg the first day.

chapter 3

BECOMING AN ATHLETIC TRAINER

Athletic trainers take different career paths, but most start with an interest in sports. Keith Abrams is a certified athletic trainer in Tampa, Florida. His path to become a trainer began after his own sports injury. He hurt his knee in a football game at Kean University in Union, New Jersey. He spent hours exercising in the athletic training room. While there, he watched the trainer at work. "The experience had a lasting impact on my life," he says.

Abrams earned a bachelor's degree in physical education. His degree included work in athletic training. After that, he continued his education. He earned a master's degree from San Jose State University.

WHAT MAKES A GOOD TRAINER?

The first step in becoming a trainer is to take a good look at yourself. Do you have what it takes?

"The most important trait an athletic trainer needs is the desire to help people," says Arizona trainer Robbie Dyson. "Each day you hear people's complaints. They tell you their aches and pains. You have to make those issues your priority."

Another important trait is flexibility, he adds. "In the traditional setting, you work with sports teams. You are part of a support

Personal trainers work in health clubs and private practice. They help people achieve fitness goals. Requirements for certification differ from those for certified athletic trainers.

staff. You must be ready to adjust to practice and game schedules that constantly change. In professional sports, you must always be available. You can get a call at any time, day or night. You need to be there for your athletes."

You also need to want to continue learning. "The trainer's education covers a broad range of health care," Dyson says. "But sometimes you need knowledge that goes deeper than what you learned in school. There are also new ways to evaluate and treat athletes. So you must take steps to continue to educate yourself. You need to commit yourself to learning, not just in school but for your whole professional career."

You also need skills that help you talk with different types of people. You need a positive personality. "You must enjoy interacting with people," Abrams says. "We work closely with coaches, athletes, and other athletic trainers. You should be friendly and outgoing. It's hard for others to get along with someone who's grumpy or unfriendly. Talking with coaches, athletic directors, general managers, the media, and more is a big part of our jobs."

Of course, it also helps to care about sports—either as a player or a fan. You also need good judgment and a sense of humor. And you must be dependable. Other good traits include problem solving, leadership, time management, and computer literacy. You also need an interest in how the body moves.

HIGH SCHOOL PROGRAMS FOR TRAINERS

Does your high school have a sports medicine program or class? Enroll in it.

Olathe North High School in Kansas has such a program. Freshmen start with a special physical education class. The class teaches how the body functions during exercise. Students also learn about the science of movement. The class covers health careers and medical terms.

Sophomores take Sports Medicine I, a first course in training. Students learn to evaluate and understand injuries. They also learn how to handle emergencies. Juniors take Sports Medicine II. The class includes first aid and CPR.

Seniors get to watch or work next to trainers in secondary schools or colleges. Or the students might choose a physical therapist or chiropractor. Another choice is working with elementary students with special needs. In the most recent program, one student teamed with a veterinarian. Another worked with a sports nutritionist.

If your school does not have such a program, take college preparatory classes in subjects like anatomy, biology, math, physiology, and psychology. You should also take health and physical education. Enroll in CPR and first-aid classes at your local hospital, Red Cross, or American Heart Association chapter. Serve a volunteer internship in a school or other sports organization. Contact health care professionals in your area. Ask if you can come along and watch them at work.

St. Francis High School in La Canada, California, also has a program for trainers. It is held through both the science and athletic departments. In 1999, its kinesiology and rehabilitation course was the first lab-science, sports medicine course approved by the University of California. Students work as rookie trainers at interscholastic games.

Seniors work as "senior" or "head" trainers for a specific sports team.

The high school also works with California State University Northridge's trainer education program. The college students learn from and help the high school's sports medicine team.

EDUCATIONAL REQUIREMENTS

If you want to be a certified athletic trainer, you first need a bachelor's degree in athletic

ANNUAL HIGH SCHOOL SPORTS MEDICINE COMPETITION

High school students in sports medicine and athletic training programs at their schools annually test their skills at the High School Sports Medicine Competition in La Canada, California. St. Francis High School hosts the contest.

The contest includes a written test and an oral presentation. It also has a practical side. The young trainers compete in a taping and wrapping challenge. Individual winners are grouped as "rookies" or "advanced." School winners are rated in the small or large school divisions. The contest sponsor also awards an annual High School Athletic Training Student of the Year.

The school's Sports Medicine Club started the contest, which is approved by the California Athletic Trainers' Association, in 2002.

training. The program must be approved by the Commission on Accreditation of Allied Health Education Programs. The program must include instruction as well as experience. Typical courses include the following:

- Prevention of sports injuries
- Evaluation of sports injuries
- First aid and emergency care
- Healing methods
- Exercise therapy
- Administration of athletic training programs
- Human anatomy
- Nutrition
- Psychology
- Personal and community health

The American Red Cross certifies children as young as eleven in cardiopulmonary resuscitation (CPR) if they pass the written exam and skills test. Hospitals and other organizations also offer classes.

The student also needs six hundred clock hours of practice. A certified athletic trainer must supervise the hours.

A list of certified college and university programs for each state is available on the NATA Web site. A bachelor's degree is the minimum requirement. Many certified athletic trainers also earn master's or even doctoral degrees.

EARNING CERTIFICATION

The Board of Certification, Inc. (BOC) began in 1989. It provides a program to certify beginning athletic trainers. The BOC creates and reviews standards for the career. The BOC has the only approved program for trainers in the United States.

The certification test has three parts. The first is a three-hour multiple-choice test. The time allows just one minute per question. The second part is a written test. Its questions

GET AN EARLY START

Are you interested in athletic training as a career? Get an early start.

"Getting involved as soon as possible will give you a huge head start in your education and career," says Arizona trainer Robbie Dyson. "Get started by observing a professional."

Contact your school's athletic trainer. Ask to watch him or her at work. Or volunteer to help. You can volunteer in a physical therapy clinic. You might even be able to get a job there as a technician. "In many states, a physical therapy tech can do a lot of hands-on work with patients," Dyson adds.

are designed to show decision-making and thinking skills. The test gives examples of events. The person who takes the test must decide which things are the most important. He or she must then create a plan for the situation.

Sample Questions

Here are some sample questions from the multiple-choice section of the Board of Certification exam for athletic trainers:

1. The athletic trainer suspects that the athlete may have an eating disorder. Which of the following actions should the athletic trainer take at this time?

Choose all that apply.

A. Allow the athlete to continue sport participation.

B. Call the athlete's parents/guardians.

C. Facilitate an initial intervention with the athlete and qualified personnel.

D. Refer the athlete to qualified medical personnel.

E. Take the athlete to the emergency room.

2. During a high school softball game, an athletic trainer notices lightning in the sky followed five seconds later by a loud clap of thunder. What action should the athletic trainer take?

Choose only one.

A. The game should be temporarily canceled.

B. The game should be postponed, and participants and spectators should leave the field.

C. The game should continue unless lightning comes closer to the field.

D. The participants should wait in the dugout.

E. The participants should seek shelter under the bleachers.

3. Twenty-four hours after a concussion was sustained, the athletic trainer reassesses the athlete using the graded symptom checklist. Based on the findings, what action should the athletic trainer take at this time?

Choose only one.

A. Allow the athlete to return to full participation in athletic activities and then reassess in twenty-four hours.

Professional golfer Natalie Gulbis of the Ladies Professional Golf Association performs a thoracic rotation exercise to stretch her torso. Flexibility is important both in preventing and rehabilitating injury.

SAMPLE QUESTIONS (CONT.)

B. Allow the athlete to return to noncontact drills only and then reassess in twenty-four hours.

C. Allow the athlete to return to play and then reassess in twenty minutes.

D. Instruct the athlete to complete twenty minutes on a stationary bike and then reassess.

E. Withhold the athlete from all athletic activities and then reassess in twenty-four hours.

The last part is a practical test. The candidate again gets a realistic event. He or she then must "treat" a live human model with an "injury." The candidate might have to check for vital signs, evaluate the injury, or show how to perform muscle testing. Or the candidate may have to show taping and wrapping skills, or all of the above.

Once a trainer is certified, the need for education doesn't end. To stay certified, a trainer must take classes, attend conferences, or consult with other athletic trainers. The BOC creates and reviews trainers' continuing education requirements. The extra learning keeps the trainer up-to-date on new developments that affect his or her career. Some employers pay for classes or conferences the trainer needs. The amount of money varies from place to place.

The certification is national, but forty-seven states also required trainers to be licensed or registered, according to the Bureau of Labor Statistics in 2009.

chapter 4

SPORTS LAW AND ETHICS

The National Athletic Trainers' Association was founded in 1950. By its account, membership grew 520 percent between 1974 and 2012. Today, it has more than thirty thousand members around the world. Some of its growth has been due to more job openings in the field. Two trends helped create those jobs. Both involved legal issues. The first was a federal law. The second was a trend in court cases.

The federal Patsy T. Mink Equal Opportunity in Education Act became law in 1972. The law is also known as Title IX. Mink was the congresswoman who wrote the bill. The act made it illegal to discriminate against women in sports. Women could no longer be left out of sports. And they had to get the same benefits and facilities as men.

Title IX created more college sports for women. More female student-athletes came to colleges. That meant more practices and more games that needed trainers—and more chances for players to get hurt. Trainers had more jobs to choose from.

LAWSUITS

The second trend involved sports-related lawsuits. The trend was a change in the focus of the suits. The number of cases where athletes sued companies that made flawed equipment was giving way to cases against the health care industry.

It's not uncommon for the one bringing a lawsuit to sue every-one in sight. This is called suing the "deep pockets." A person or organization with deep pockets is one with a lot of money. A law-suit may start with the person responsible for the harm. But the

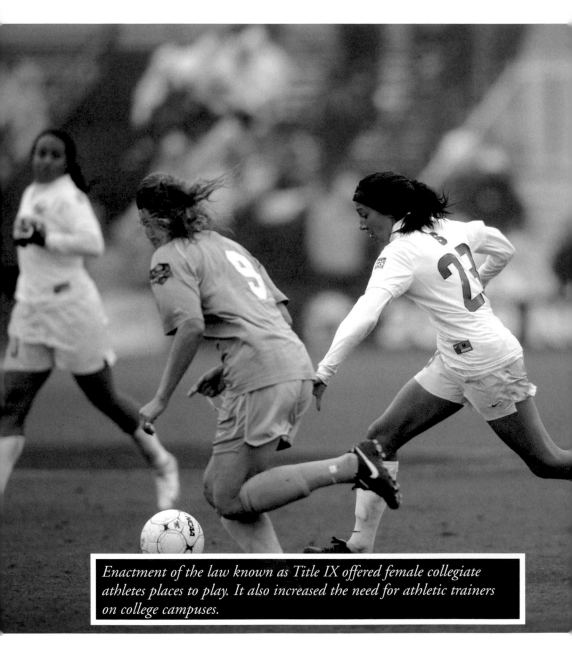

Enactment of the law known as Title IX offered female collegiate athletes places to play. It also increased the need for athletic trainers on college campuses.

suit may be filed against the school, coaches, doctors, trainers, and even teammates. Trainers may not have big bank accounts, but they can still be swept into court with everyone else.

A sports injury can result in severe disability or even death.

Sometimes the bad result is due to an error by a doctor or other health care provider. The player or the player's family may be angry and want to blame someone. Or they may need a way to pay medical bills. The next stop can be a court of law. They may file a lawsuit. Some cases are for failure to warn, failure to act, and failure to provide adequate coverage.

Coaches and trainers must tell players the risks and dangers of the sport. The players must understand them before deciding to play. If someone gets hurt without being notified, he or she can sue. The case will charge "failure to warn."

"Failure to act" is another legal issue. It applies to a person who knows a rule and ignores it. For instance, the governing body for U.S. swimming requires that coaches teach racing dives in deep water. But what if a coach teaches a swimmer to dive in the shallow end? The swimmer may hit his or her head on the bottom of the pool and get a brain injury. The coach may be charged with "failure to act."

American swimming coaches are required to teach racing dives in deep water. A coach who ignores the rule can be charged with "failure to act" if a swimmer is injured.

REASONABLE CARE

Lawsuits may also claim "failure to provide adequate medical coverage." "Adequate" means, in part, the number of trainers the school or organization hires. Such a case claims negligence. Negligence is failure to use reasonable care. The failure hurts another.

In one lawsuit, a football player got hurt in a game. The team doctor let others move him from the field. They carried him without a stretcher, and the player became paralyzed. The court ruled that the doctor's action was wrong. It found the doctor at fault.

The NATA addressed the issue in its 2003 revision of the Recommendations and Guidelines for the Appropriate Medical Coverage of Intercollegiate Athletics. The guidelines first appeared in 2000.

The NATA helped define "adequate care" as the term applies to trainers. It created a way to figure out how many trainers a school or organization needs. The method includes the number of sports offered, the risks of injury for each sport, and how many facilities are involved. Schools that used the NATA guide created so many jobs that the career began to attract women. Before that, most trainers were men.

CAREER WOMEN

At first, female trainers worked with women's sports. Some ventured into men's track and field. By the late 1980s, women finally worked with football players at the college level. More than ten years passed before the National Football League (NFL) hired its first full-time female trainer. In 2002, Arika Iso joined the Pittsburg Steelers as an assistant trainer. No women became head trainers in the NFL, though. However, 70 percent of the head trainers in the Women's National Basketball Association (WNBA) are female, according to Livestrong.com.

LANDMARK COURT CASE

In 1975, a sophomore football player in Seattle, Washington, got hurt in a game. He lowered his head when another player tried to tackle him. The hit broke a bone in his spine. The case went to court. It was called *Thompson v. Seattle Public School District.*

Before this case, few people thought that telling players about dangers of sports was important. In fact, many never thought of it at all. But in 1985, the court found the coach and school district at fault for failing to warn the student about risks.

The court ordered them to pay the player $6.3 million. Today, coaches must make sure that players and parents understand the dangers of playing each sport. Players may have to sign a form that says they have been told and understand the risks.

The Los Angeles Dodgers hired Sue Falsone in 2011. She was the first female head athletic trainer in Major League Baseball. She was also the first female head trainer in a major professional sport for men.

PRIVACY LAWS

Trainers must obey the same laws as doctors and other health care professionals. One such law is the federal Health Insurance Portability and Accountability Act of 1996 (HIPAA). The Privacy Rule is part of this law. It states who can know a patient's health information. The rule applies to all data: oral, written, and electronic. Protected information includes conversations, medical records, computer data, and more.

"The law limits the ways trainers talk with the athlete, the doctor, and parents," says sports trainer Wayne Harmon. "Doctors can't talk to me without a waiver."

A waiver gives up a right. The waiver must be voluntary, and it must be signed on purpose. An injured player must waive his or her right to privacy. That gives doctors permission to talk to the trainer. The trainer also needs permission to talk to

When the Los Angeles Dodgers hired Sue Falsone as head athletic trainer in 2011, she was the first female head trainer in a major league professional sport for men.

others. The law makes it a bit hard to share facts about a player's injury—even with other sports medicine workers.

The first sports medicine diagnosis in the United States was "traumatic arthritis," suffered by Los Angeles Dodgers fastball pitcher Sandy Koufax in 1964.

THE FIRST U.S. SPORTS MEDICINE DIAGNOSIS

Los Angeles Dodgers pitcher Sandy Koufax was known for his fastball. Doctors said he wasn't built to be a pitcher. His muscles were too big. But at the time, no trainers were on hand. If players got hurt, they lived with the pain.

Koufax hurt his left elbow in a game in 1964. He jammed it when he dove into second base to beat a pickoff throw. Weeks later, doctors diagnosed the three-time Cy Young winner with traumatic arthritis. Arthritis is swelling that leads to changes in a joint. Koufax's type was caused by an acute injury.

He treated himself with ice and a lotion he made from hot peppers that burned his skin. Despite the pain, he set a major league pitching record that year.

Other Legal Issues

Trainers must know about other legal issues. One is called informed consent. Informed consent occurs after a conversation between a doctor and patient—or a trainer and patient. The consent is the patient's OK for a medical procedure. It often applies to surgery, but it can refer to other treatments, too.

Informed consent has three parts: information, understanding, and voluntary agreement. The patient must be told what the possible treatment is for. He or she must also learn what the treatment is like. The doctor must present any other possible choices of treatment. The doctor must also discuss risks and benefits of all the choices. Of course, any risks that may apply to permanent disability or life-threatening results must be told. The talk must also include the risks and benefits of refusing the procedure. This part of informed consent has another side for athletes. The doctor must talk about both the short-term and long-term risks of playing sports with the medical condition.

The patient must be able to understand what the doctor says. That means the information must be clear and free of highly technical words. The doctor also cannot try to persuade or force the patient to agree to the treatment.

Sometimes athletes insist on playing even when doctors think they should sit out. This is called making a decision against medical advice. In such cases, the health care professional must explain the risks and benefits of playing with the injury. The player must assume all of the risks. He or she must sign a risk waiver and release form.

NATA Code of Ethics

A code of ethics is a list of behaviors that members of a profession follow. It creates and maintains high standards for the career. The NATA has one for athletic trainers. It includes four main principles:

1. Respect the rights, welfare, and dignity of all.
2. Obey laws and regulations.
3. Maintain and promote high standards.
4. Avoid bad behavior.

The first principle means trainers cannot discriminate against people based on race, color, national origin, age, sex, gender identity, and more. Members must provide competent care. They must also keep medical data private.

The second principle includes all local, state, and federal laws. Trainers must also obey guidelines of the places they work. Trainers must follow NATA rules. And they must report illegal or unethical practices by others. Finally, trainers must avoid abuse of alcohol and other drugs. They must seek treatment if they develop a problem.

According to principle three, NATA members must be honest about their identities, skills, training, credentials, and services they provide. They must provide only the services they are qualified for. They must also provide, refer, or seek fees only for services the patient needs. Members must continue their education throughout their careers. If they are in charge of other trainers, members must tell them about the code of ethics. Trainers who teach or do research must use ethical conduct in those activities.

The fourth principle deals with behavior. Members' conduct must reflect on the profession in a positive way. They cannot use the NATA logo to endorse products or services. They must never take advantage of a patient to make money. And they must never use information they get in the course of their work to affect the score or outcome of a game or for gambling.

The code of ethics doesn't cover every situation that a trainer may meet. But it guides trainers' actions.

chapter 5

THE JOB OUTLOOK

Many athletic trainers work for sports teams at all levels, from youth to the pros. They also work with people of all ages in such places as industrial and commercial settings, the armed forces, law enforcement, and the performing arts.

Athletic training is an allied health profession. Allied health professions involve the prevention, identification, and evaluation of diseases and disorders. Professionals have formal education and clinical training. And they have qualified to become certified, registered, or licensed. An allied health professional teams up with doctors and other health care practitioners to deliver patient care.

The services an athletic trainer can provide, as well as the type of supervision required, are determined by the states. In some states, athletic trainers provide services on their own. In others, their treatments must be approved by a doctor or licensed physical therapist.

In 2011, the Bureau of Labor Statistics stated that job opportunities for athletic trainers would grow 37 percent between 2008 and 2018. That growth is much faster than the average expected for other occupations. The rise is due in part to the prevention part of the job. Injury prevention keeps health care costs low.

The bureau said most new jobs will be in hospitals and offices of doctors and other health care workers. Other jobs will open at fitness and recreation centers. Jobs with high

Patient education will continue to be an important part of the athletic trainer's job in the future. The services that trainers provide are increasing. That means more job opportunities for trainers.

school teams are also likely to increase. In some states, people are working to get a trainer in every high school. Most professional and collegiate sports teams already have complete training staffs. Landing a job there will be more competitive.

Trainers continue to offer more services. That helps them find jobs for more money or different places to work. In 2008, the Bureau of Labor Statistics stated that 38 percent of athletic trainers worked in hospitals and medical offices. In hospitals, trainers work in outpatient rehabilitation and wellness clinics. In doctors' offices, they work as "physician extenders." A physician extender is a health care worker. He or she is not a doctor but performs some of the same tasks as doctors. In sports medicine, these jobs are in family practice, pediatrics, orthopedics, and other specialties.

In those places, trainers take patient histories, evaluate injuries, and teach patients the exercises the doctor recommends. They also provide general patient education. Trainers in these offices help more patients get care in the same amount of time needed for doctors working alone. The increase pays off, as the office gets more money.

JOBS IN INDUSTRY

Trainers also work in industry. For example, both General Motors and the Ford Motor Company have employed trainers to keep assembly-line workers healthy. Those workers routinely repeat the same motions.

Trainers in the workplace look for the causes of injuries. They create injury prevention programs; run back-to-work programs; and teach about health, nutrition, fitness, and wellness. Some trainers serve as safety officers. They perform the same triage and immediate treatment duties that they would use on an athletic field. And they may perform

As the older population places more emphasis on fitness, more opportunities exist for athletic trainers who can help older athletes prevent and rehabilitate sports injuries.

HOW I BECAME A CERTIFIED ATHLETIC TRAINER

Robbie Dyson of Arizona has worked as a certified athletic trainer in professional football and baseball. He has also worked in colleges and high schools and in clinics.

"I've always loved sports," he says. "Both competing in them and watching them. And at some point in high school, I realized I had a special interest in medicine."

Dyson chose the University of Kansas because it had both athletic training and pre-physical therapy programs. "When I enrolled, I was unsure which I would pursue," he says. "I soon chose the athletic training program. After graduation I passed the certification exam so I could practice as an athletic trainer."

PUBLIC SAFETY AND MILITARY JOBS

Athletic trainers also work in public safety jobs. Police and fire academies and departments want their police officers and firefighters to stay fit. Trainers in this field provide injury prevention, treatment, rehab, reconditioning, and health education.

Trainers also have a place in the armed forces. Athletic training is not a military job, but the military hires civilian trainers. Some trainers work for the armed forces in the federal civil service system. The U.S. Marine Corps needs training for its community services Semper Fit program. This program includes sports, recreation, health promotion, and fitness and recreational safety. The U.S. Navy hires trainers for its Morale, Welfare, and Recreation

health checks and physicals before the company hires a new worker.

System. The navy also hires trainers to create fitness programs for the Navy Seals. And the U.S. Coast Guard uses trainers at its Initial Training Center in Cape May, New Jersey.

THE PERFORMING ARTS

Dancers and other performers risk the same kinds of injuries as athletes. Athletic trainers have been working with such artists for more than twenty-five years. Performers need strength conditioning and injury prevention. They also need treatment when they get hurt. The Blue Man Group, the Cincinnati Ballet, Cirque du Soleil, Disneyland, Disney World, the Radio City Music Hall Rockettes, and the Pittsburgh Ballet Theater all use trainers for their performers.

Musicians risk injury from repeated motion. They, too, benefit from the services of athletic trainers. Violinists, for example, can get tennis elbow, the same condition that tennis players get. The condition may be due to overuse. Stretching exercises both prevent and relieve the condition. So symphony orchestras hire trainers, too.

GETTING AHEAD

Keith Abrams of Florida began his career working for professional sports. During graduate school, he worked for the Salinas Peppers, a minor league baseball team in California. He soon took a job with an Atlanta Braves minor league team. He moved on to the National Football League with the Tampa Bay Buccaneers.

"After five years, I took a chance with the XFL," Abrams says. He was head athletic trainer for the New Jersey Hitmen. The pro football league lasted only one season. But he had gained enough experience to land a job with the Kansas City

Some athletic trainers think working in the National Football League is a dream job. But success depends on what the trainer wants to do and where he or she wants to work.

Chiefs and head coach Dick Vermeil. Abrams says making contacts and hard work are the best ways to advance in an athletic training career.

"I hate to say this but it's really who you know and not what you know," Abrams says. "All athletic trainers are nationally certified. A lot of us have advanced degrees. So in theory, anyone should be able to work for the Chiefs. I was fortunate to have a very strong connection to Coach Vermeil. So I got the job."

Hard work is also important. "We work very hard and can't afford to pull the weight of a lazy trainer," he says. "So it's important to work hard and be seen as someone who takes pride in his or her work."

Moving up the ranks means different things to different people. "Most athletic trainers view the professional level, especially the National Football League, as the job of all jobs," Abrams says. "So they strive to reach that level. Almost 90 percent of the female trainers I know want to work there. Other trainers are happy working at Division I colleges.

WHAT'S A PERSONAL TRAINER?

If you go to a health club, you might use the services of a personal trainer. Personal trainers help people achieve their fitness goals. The skill set for this job includes the ability to design safe and effective exercise programs for clients.

Personal trainers need knowledge of the basic sciences, but they have no higher education requirements in the health sciences. Personal trainers must know the role of injury or illness in planning a program, but they don't need to know how to identify or treat them.

The National Academy of Sports Medicine (NASM) and the American Council on Exercise (ACE) offer certification tests. Candidates for the entry-level ACE certification must be at least eighteen years old and be trained in CPR.

Still others like their jobs at the high school level or in a clinic. Training eats away at your personal time. It just depends on what they are willing to do to reach their goals."

Getting ahead is in the eye of the beholder. "Advancement depends on where you want to be and where you want to work," says Wayne Harmon.

The Bureau of Labor Statistics says there are several ways trainers can get ahead in their careers. Some assistants move up to head trainers. Trainers can also move into management roles. They direct at doctors' offices, hospitals, or clinics.

Some switch teams or sports to move up. The new jobs may add more duties or pay more. Trainers can also move into sales jobs. They use their knowledge to sell medical or athletic equipment.

Or they can start their own businesses. Abrams started a company called Athletic Trainer 4 Hire. It's a free, nationwide job-listing service. It gives leaders of sporting events and camps a quick, easy way to find trainers. "My company started in 2008," he says. "Four years later, I dedicated 100 percent of my time and effort to build it. That's when I began seeing results. I'm a small and humble company just trying to make a difference."

REWARDS

Like many careers, training has its share of rewards and challenges. "The best part of the career is helping athletes return to sports after an injury," Abrams says. "I think any athletic trainer would agree with me."

Abrams watched from the sideline as Kansas City Chiefs running back Priest Holmes scored a touchdown. The score was his twenty-seventh of the season. It won him the single season rushing touchdown record in 2003.

"Words can't explain the joy trainers feel when their athletes and teams do well from all of their hard work," he says. "It's a great feeling. I absolutely love my profession and the ability to interact with coaches and players on a daily basis."

Wayne Harmon likes the detective part of the job. For example, a quarterback falls. Did he get kicked? Hit with equipment? Or faint?

"Why did he get hurt?" asks Harmon. "What else goes with it? This job keeps you learning. There's always something new and different. You always have to be an adult learner."

CHALLENGES

An athletic trainer's job isn't easy. "One of the biggest challenges is the time needed for the job," says Abrams. "In general, trainers work long hours. And they don't always get paid

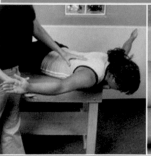
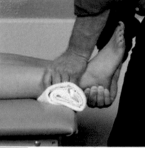
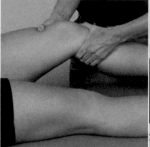

AthleticTrainer4Hire.com

LICENSED. CERTIFIED. QUAL

MEDCO
SPORTS MEDICINE

LOGIN

User Name [_____]

Password [_____]

(Login) (Reset)

CLICK HERE TO RENEW!

 STOP SPORTS INJURIES | PARTICIPATING MEDICAL INSTITUTION/ PRACTICE

AIR DOMINION
Dominate the Game

Welcome to Athletictrainer4hire.com!
Your Nationwide Network of Certified Athletic Trainers

Event Coordinators

Why Join?

- **FREE** Registration and we'll find the Athletic Trainer for you
- Over 30,000 Certified Athletic Trainers nationwide
- Quick & Easy job listings at your fingertips
- Certified and qualified medical professions
- Athletic trainers from your community

Click here

Athletic Trainers

Why Join?

- Make **EXTRA** money while doing the job you enjoy
- Unlimited earning potential for a low annual membership fee
- We bring the jobs to you with **FREE** preview of job listings
- Receive instant email alerts of job listings in your area
- Save with discounts of various products

Click here

AthleticTrainer4Hire.com was created to help event coordinators and certified athleti trainers make contact about upcoming sporting events and sports camps. Many spor events across the world go without medical coverage or supervision on a regular bas With this website, finding certified athletic trainers or locating upcoming sporting eve is made much easier. All you would need to do is simply register and list your availab positions, or register and begin scrolling through the available positions for your nex sporting event. It's that simple!

Hire Certified Athletic Trainers for Your Next Event

The athletic trainers available on this website will be certified by the Board of

AthleticTrainer4Hire.com is a private business begun by an athletic trainer. It's a free, nationwide job-listing service. It's an easy way to find trainers to hire for sporting events and camps.

enough for their work. The hours in the training room and traveling take away from personal time with family or friends. The long hours and low pay have caused many trainers to seek other careers."

Robbie Dyson of Arizona agrees. "Most sports events occur in the afternoon and evening on weekdays and weekends," he says. "So your workday can end late at night. And your weekends can be busy with work."

For him, though, perhaps the best part of the job is when he's not working at all. "I watch sports for a living," he says. "And if I'm not working, everyone is happy! If everyone stays healthy and there are no injuries, then the player is happy, coach is happy, Mom and Dad are happy."

And the athletic trainer is happy!

glossary

acute injury A sudden injury.

allied health professional A health care practitioner involved in the prevention, identification, and evaluation of diseases and disorders. The profession requires formal education and clinical training, as well as certification, registration, or licensure.

capillary refill The time blood takes to return to the fingertip after pressure on the fingernail is applied and released.

chronic injury An injury that develops over time due to overuse or repetitive motion.

code of ethics A list of behaviors that members of a professional follow.

compression Squeezing or pressing together of a body area, often to remove liquids.

crisis plan An emergency care plan put in place prior to injury.

informed consent Communication between a doctor and patient that results in the patient's agreement to a medical procedure.

liable Responsible or at fault for injury to another.

ligament Body tissue that connects bone to bone.

medical history A record of past and present health.

negligence Failure to provide reasonable care, resulting in harm or injury to another.

open surgery Traditional surgery that requires a cut large enough for the surgeon to see the body part and insert instruments.

physician extender A health care professional who performs services typically performed by a doctor.

primary assessment A check for life-threatening injuries to the airway, breathing, and circulation.

secondary assessment A check for injuries that are not life threatening.

sprain A tear or stretching of a muscle or tendon.

strain A tear or stretching of a ligament.

tendon The part of a muscle that attaches to a bone.

triage Sorting patients according to severity of injury to determine the order in which each is treated.

waiver The giving up of a right. The act must be voluntary and intentional.

for more information

Canadian Academy of Sport and Exercise Medicine
180 Elgin Street, Suite 1400
Ottawa, ON K2P 2K3
Canada
(613) 748-5851
E-mail: admin@casem-acmse.org
Web site: http://www.casm-acms.org
The Canadian Academy of Sport and Exercise Medicine is an
organization of physicians in the practice of medicine as it
applies to physical athletic training. It seeks to advance the
art and science of sports medicine.

Canadian Athletic Therapists Association (CATA)
1040 7th Avenue SW, Suite 402
Calgary, AB T2P 3G9
Canada
(403) 509-2282
E-mail: info@athletictherapy.org
Web site: http://www.athletictherapy.org
This nonprofit organization promotes delivery of high-quality
injury prevention, emergency services, and rehabilitation
for athletic trainers and members of the community, as
well as high-performance athletes.

College Athletic Trainers' Society
Dinsmore & Shohl, LLP
One Oxford Centre
301 Grant Street, Suite 2800
Pittsburgh, PA 15219

E-mail: jlee@collegeathletictrainer.org
Web site: http://www.collegeathletictrainer.org
The College Athletic Trainers' Society was founded to promote high-quality care for student-athletes and provide education and career development opportunities for athletic trainers at colleges and universities.

Health Professionals Network (HPN)
P.O. Box 2007
Midlothian, VA 23113
(804) 639-9211
E-mail: info@healthpronet.org
Web site: http://www.healthpronet.org
The HPN is a group of national organizations that represent two hundred of the leading health professions. Membership includes associations, accrediting agencies, educational institutions, and licensing and certification bodies.

International Federation of Sports Medicine
La Maison du Sport International
Av Rhodanie
Kiewitstraat 141
3500 Hasselt
Lausanne, Switzerland
Web site: http://www.fims.org
The International Federation of Sports Medicine is a worldwide association committed to the study and development of sports medicine. It offers courses, publication of scientific information, and international meetings.

National Athletic Trainers' Association (NATA)
2952 Stemmons Freeway, #200
Dallas, TX 75247

(214) 637-6282

Web site: http://www.nata.org

The NATA is the professional association for certified athletic
trainers. Its goal is to enhance the services provided by
certified athletic trainers and advance the profession of
athletic training.

National Center for Catastrophic Sport Injury Research

Department of Exercise and Sport Science CB# 8700

209 Fetzer Gymnasium

University of North Carolina at Chapel Hill

Chapel Hill, NC 27599

(919) 962-5171

E-mail: mueller@email.unc.edu

Web site: http://www.unc.edu/depts/nccsi

The National Center for Catastrophic Sport Injury Research
collects and distributes information about sports brain
and/or spinal cord injuries that involve death or permanent disability. The National Collegiate Athletic
Association, the American Football Coaches Association,
and the National Federation of State High School
Associations fund the research.

National Collegiate Athletic Association (NCAA)

700 W. Washington Street

P.O. Box 6222

Indianapolis, IN 46206-6222

(317) 917-6222

Web site: http://www.ncaa.org

The NCAA governs competition at the college and university
level. Its goal is to encourage fair, safe, and sportsmanlike
competition. It also seeks to enhance student-athletes'
educational experience.

National Strength and Conditioning Association (NSCA)
1885 Bob Johnson Drive
Colorado Springs, CO 80906
(719) 632-6722
E-mail: nsca@nsca-lift.org
Web site: http://www.nsca-lift.org
The NSCA is an international authority on strength and
    conditioning. It supports and disseminates research-based
    information to improve athletic performance and fitness.

World Federation of Athletic Training and Therapy
Department of Health & Kinesiology
Purdue University
800 W. Stadium Avenue
West Lafayette, IN 47907
(765) 494-3167
Web site: http://www.wfatt.org
The World Federation of Athletic Training and Therapy is a
    group of national organizations of sports medicine health
    care professionals who treat and work to prevent injury
    and illness in the fields of sports and exercise.

WEB SITES

Due to the changing nature of Internet links, Rosen Publishing
has developed an online list of Web sites related to the subject
of this book. This site is updated regularly. Please use this link
to access the list:

http://www.rosenlinks.com/ECAR/Train

for further reading

Bellenir, Karen. *Sports Injuries Information for Teens: Health Tips About Acute, Traumatic, and Chronic Injuries in Adolescent Athletes* (Teen Health Series). Detroit, MI: Omnigraphics, 2008.

Chisolm, Stephanie. *The Health Professions: Trends and Opportunities in U.S. Health.* Sudbury, MA: Jones & Bartlett Publishers, 2007.

Culverhouse, Gay. *Throwaway Players: Concussion Crisis from Pee Wee Football to the NFL.* Lake Forest, CA: Behler Publications, 2011.

Fehler, Gene. *Beanball.* New York, NY: Clarion Books, 2011.

Furgang, Kathy. *Frequently Asked Questions About Sports Injuries.* (FAQ: Teen Life). New York, NY: Rosen Publishing, 2008.

Gatz, Greg. *Complete Conditioning for Soccer.* Champaign, IL: Human Kinetics, 2009.

Headley, Justina Chen. *Girl Overboard.* New York, NY: Little, Brown and Company, 2008.

Ivey, Pat, and Josh Stoner. *Complete Conditioning for Football.* Champaign, IL: Human Kinetics, 2011.

Kamberg, Mary-Lane. *Headlines! Sports Concussions.* New York, NY: Rosen Publishing, 2011.

Katovsky, Bill, and Peter Larson. *Tread Lightly: Evolution, Footwear Innovation, and the Quest for Injury-Free Running.* New York, NY: Skyhorse Publishing, 2012.

Liberman, Art, Randy Brown, and Eileen Myers. *The Everything Running Book.* Avon, MA: Adams Media, 2012.

Lore, Nicholas. *Now What?: The Young Person's Guide to Choosing the Perfect Career.* New York, NY: Fireside, 2008.

Perrin, David. *Athletic Taping and Bracing.* Champaign, IL: Human Kinetics, 2012.

Rue, Nancy. *Tournaments, Cocoa, and One Wrong Move.* Grand Rapids, MI: Zondervan, 2011.

Thomas, Craig Angle. *How to Raise a Successful Athlete.* Victoria, BC, Canada: Trafford Publishing, 2006.

Thygerson, Alton L. *Sports First Aid and Injury Prevention.* Sudbury, MA: Jones & Bartlett Publishers, 2008.

bibliography

American Academy of Orthopaedic Surgeons. "Knee Arthroscopy." OrthoInfo, March 2010. Retrieved January 30, 2012 (http://orthoinfo.aaos.org/topic. cfm?topic=a00299).

Arthritis Health Center. "Arthroscopy." WebMD.com, January 7, 2011. Retrieved January 30, 2012 (http:// arthritis.webmd.com/arthroscopy-surgical-procedure).

Board of Certification for the Athletic Trainer. "Sample Exam Questions." 2011. Retrieved January 28, 2012. (http://www.bocatc.org/index.php?option=com_content &view=article&id=107&Itemid=115).

Bureau of Labor Statistics. "Athletic Trainers." *Occupational Outlook Handbook, 2010–2011 Edition.* Retrieved December 10, 2011 (http://www.bls.gov/oco/ocos294.htm).

Carnes, David. "Definition of Sport Psychology." Livestrong.com, May 3, 2011. Retrieved January 19, 2012 (http://www.livestrong.com/ article/134188-definition-sport-psychology).

Cartwright, Loren A., and William A. Pitney. *Fundamentals of Athletic Training.* Champaign, IL: Human Kinetics, 2011.

Chain Drug Review. "Children's Sports Injuries on Rise." Vol. 33, No. 13, August 8, 2011, p. 22. Retrieved

January 30, 2012 (http://go.galegroup.com.ezproxy.
jocolibrary.org/ps/i.do?id=GALE%7CA265194948&v=
2.1&u=jcl_cen&it=r&p=ITOF&sw=w).

Clover, Jim. *Sports Medicine Essentials: Core Concepts in
Athletic Training and Fitness Instruction.* Clifton Park,
NY: Thomson Delmar Learning, 2007.

ExploreHealthCareers.org. "Do Something That Matters.
For Yourself. For Others. Athletic Trainer." Retrieved
January 24, 2012 (http://explorehealth careers.org/en/
Career/57/Athletic_Trainer).

Georgoulis, A.D., I.S. Kiapidou, L. Velogianni, N.
Stergiou, and A. Boland. "Herodicus, the Father of
Sports Medicine." *Knee Surgery Sports Traumatol
Arthroscopy*, Vol. 15, No. 3, March, 2007, pp. 315–318.
Retrieved January 30, 2012. (http://www.ncbi.nlm.nih.
gov/pubmed/16951976).

Hartley-Parkinson, Richard. "Children Flee in Terror as
Roof Collapses onto Ice Hockey Rink as They Are
Training." Mail Online, January 29, 2012. Retrieved
January 29, 2012. (http://www.dailymail.co.uk/news/
article-2091782/Children-flee-terror-roof-collapses-ice-
hockey-rink-training.html#ixzz1kt3wwXo5http://www.
dailymail.co.uk/news/article-2091782/Children-flee-
terror-roof-collapses-ice-hockey-rink-training.
html#ixzz1kt3wwXo5).

Hootman, Jennifer M., Dick Randall, and Julie Agel.
"Epidemiology of Collegiate Injuries for 15 Sports:
Summary and Recommendations for Injury Prevention

Initiatives." *Journal of Athletic Training*, April–June 2007. Retrieved January 26, 2012. (http://www.ncbi. nlm.nih.gov/pmc/articles/PMC1941297).

Kent, Linda Tarr. "Females in Athletic Training." Livestrong.com, May 26, 2011. Retrieved February 3, 2012 (http://www.livestrong.com/ article/370326-females-in-athletic-training).

McCullough, J. Bradley. "Hurts So Good." *Kansas City Star*, December 11, 2011, pp. D4–D6.

Minigh, Jennifer L. *Sports Medicine.* Westport, CT: Greenwood Press, 2007.

National Athletic Trainers' Association. "Athletic Training Services." January 2010. Retrieved January 26, 2012 (http://www.nata.org/sites/default/files/ GuideToAthleticTrainingServices.pdf).

National Institute of Arthritis and Musculoskeletal and Skin Diseases. "Handout on Health: Sports Injuries." April 2009. Retrieved January 29, 2012. (http://www. niams.nih.gov/Health_Info/Sports_Injuries/default.asp).

Society for the Advancement of Education. "Injured Youngsters Need to Stay Involved." *USA Today*, February 2010, p. 12. Retrieved January 30, 2012 (http://findarticles.com/p/articles/mi_m1272/ is_2777_138/ai_n57059039).

Starting a Personal Training Business. "Career as Athletic Trainers." 2009. Retrieved December 10, 2011 (http://

www.starting-a-personal-training-business.com/career-as-athletic-trainers.html).

Stein, Jeannine. "Sue Falsone: Major League Baseball's First Female Head Athletic Trainer." *Los Angeles Times*, November 1, 2011. Retrieved February 3, 2012 (http://articles.latimes.com/2011/nov/01/news/la-heb-female-athletic-trainerdodgers-20111101).

USA Today. "Kansas City Running Back Priest Holmes Retires." November 23, 2007. Retrieved January 31, 2012 (http://www.usatoday.com/sports/football/nfl/chiefs/2007-11-21-holmes_N.htm).

U.S. Department of Health and Human Services. "Health Information Privacy." Retrieved February 3, 2012 (http://www.hhs.gov/ocr/privacy).

index

ABOUT THE AUTHOR

Mary-Lane Kamberg is the author of several books for Rosen Publishing. She has written magazine articles about health and sports medicine for children and adults. As a swimming coach for the Kansas City Blazers, she works with young athletes. She is certified in first aid, CPR, and safety training for swim coaches.

PHOTO CREDITS

Cover (trainer) StockLife/Shutterstock.com; cover (background), p.1 © iStockphoto.com/Tom Hahn; pp. 4, 8–9, 42–43, 58–59 © AP Images; pp. 6–7 © 2007 NBA Entertainment. Photo by Joe Murphy/NBAE/Getty Images; pp. 10–11 Chris Trotman/Getty Images; pp. 12–13 © 2007 NBA Entertainment. Photo by Andrew D. Bernstein/NBAE/ Getty Images; pp. 16–17 © 2009 NBA Entertainment. Photo by Nathaniel S. Butler/NBAE/Getty Images; p. 21 Jamie Sabau/Getty Images; pp. 24–25 Wolfgang Poelzer/WaterFrame/ Getty Images; p. 27 Peter Dazeley/Photographer's Choice/ Getty Images; p. 29 Alvis Upitis/Brand X Pictures/Getty Images; pp. 32–33 i love images/Cultura/Getty Images; p. 36 Lisa F. Young/Shutterstock.com; p. 39 Victor Decolongon/ Getty Images; p. 44 Al Bello/Getty Images; p. 47 Rick Scuteri/ Reuters/Landov; pp. 48–49 Focus On Sport/Getty Images; p. 53 Peter Muller/Cultura/Getty Images; p. 55 Sven Hagolani/ Getty Images; p. 62 © www.athletictrainer4hire.com; back cover © iStockphoto.com/blackred

Designer: Matt Cauli; Editor: Bethany Bryan;
Photo Researcher: Marty Levick